Disruptive Innovators How Technology Entrepreneurs Are Changing the World

Gabriela

Copyright © [2023]

Title: Disruptive Innovators How Technology Entrepreneurs Are Changing the World

Author's: Gabriela.

This book was printed and published by [Publisher's: Gabriela] in [2023]

ISBN:

TABLE OF CONTENTS

Chapter 1: Introduction

The Era of Disruptive Innovation

In today's fast-paced world, we find ourselves in the midst of an era of disruptive innovation. Technology entrepreneurs are revolutionizing industries, challenging the status quo, and changing the way we live and work. This subchapter explores the transformative power of disruptive innovation and its impact on various sectors, making it a must-read for anyone interested in entrepreneurship and innovation.

Disruptive innovation refers to the process through which new technologies, products, or services disrupt existing markets and create entirely new ones. It is a force that transforms industries, displaces established players, and enables entrepreneurs to redefine the rules of the game. The era of disruptive innovation has brought about groundbreaking advancements that have reshaped our lives in unimaginable ways.

One of the key characteristics of disruptive innovation is its ability to democratize access to products and services. Technology entrepreneurs have leveraged the power of the internet and mobile devices to reach customers on a global scale, bypassing traditional barriers to entry. This has opened up opportunities for aspiring entrepreneurs to enter markets that were once dominated by established players. Now, anyone with a brilliant idea and the right skills can disrupt an industry and change the world.

Disruptive innovation has had a profound impact on several sectors. Take transportation, for example. Companies like Uber and Lyft have revolutionized the way we travel, challenging traditional taxi services and creating a new on-demand model. Similarly, Airbnb disrupted the hospitality industry by providing an alternative to traditional hotels, allowing individuals to monetize their unused spaces.

The era of disruptive innovation has also transformed the healthcare industry. From wearable devices that track our vital signs to telemedicine platforms that connect patients with doctors remotely, technology entrepreneurs have made healthcare more accessible and personalized.

Education is another sector that has experienced disruptive innovation. Online learning platforms like Coursera and Udemy have democratized education, allowing anyone with an internet connection to access high-quality courses from top universities and experts.

In conclusion, the era of disruptive innovation is characterized by the relentless pursuit of breakthrough ideas and the ability to challenge established norms. Technology entrepreneurs are driving change across industries, creating new opportunities, and reshaping the world as we know it. Whether you are an aspiring entrepreneur or simply interested in the impact of innovation, understanding the era of disruptive innovation is essential for navigating the ever-evolving landscape of entrepreneurship and innovation.

The Impact of Technology Entrepreneurship

In today's fast-paced world, technology entrepreneurship has become a driving force behind the rapid transformation of various industries. This subchapter aims to shed light on the profound impact that technology entrepreneurs have on our society, addressing the audience of "everyone" with a particular focus on the niches of entrepreneurship and innovation.

Technology entrepreneurs are known for their ability to identify market gaps and develop innovative solutions that disrupt traditional industries. They possess the skills and mindset required to transform ideas into successful businesses, leveraging technology as a catalyst for change. Their impact is felt across various sectors, including healthcare, finance, transportation, and education.

One of the key impacts of technology entrepreneurship is the creation of new jobs and economic growth. By introducing disruptive technologies and business models, entrepreneurs open up opportunities for employment, both directly within their ventures and indirectly in supporting industries. This job creation not only fuels economic growth but also enables individuals to develop new skills and contribute to the advancement of society.

Furthermore, technology entrepreneurship has the power to democratize access to goods and services. Through the use of innovative technologies, entrepreneurs can reach underserved populations and provide solutions that were previously inaccessible or unaffordable. For instance, mobile banking has revolutionized financial services in developing countries, enabling individuals to access banking services without the need for physical branches.

In addition to democratization, technology entrepreneurship drives efficiency and productivity gains. By leveraging automation, data analytics, and artificial intelligence, entrepreneurs optimize processes, reduce costs, and improve the quality of products and services. This enhanced efficiency benefits both businesses and consumers, leading to increased competitiveness and improved customer experiences.

Moreover, technology entrepreneurship fosters a culture of innovation and collaboration. Entrepreneurs often collaborate with experts from diverse fields, such as scientists, engineers, and designers, to develop groundbreaking solutions. This cross-pollination of ideas and expertise accelerates the pace of innovation and encourages others to think creatively and take risks.

However, the impact of technology entrepreneurship is not without challenges. The rapid pace of technological advancements can create disruptions and uncertainties, requiring individuals and organizations to adapt quickly. Additionally, ethical considerations surrounding data privacy, cybersecurity, and the responsible use of emerging technologies must be addressed to ensure the long-term positive impact of technology entrepreneurship.

In conclusion, technology entrepreneurship is a powerful force that drives economic growth, democratizes access to goods and services, improves efficiency, and fosters innovation and collaboration. It has the potential to transform industries and change the world as we know it. As individuals and society, we must embrace and support technology entrepreneurs to harness the full potential of their impact and ensure a prosperous and inclusive future.

Chapter 2: Understanding Technology Entrepreneurship

Definition and Characteristics of Technology Entrepreneurship

Technology entrepreneurship is a rapidly growing field that has been transforming industries and shaping the world we live in. In this subchapter, we will dive into the definition and characteristics of technology entrepreneurship, aiming to provide a comprehensive understanding of its essence and relevance in today's business landscape.

At its core, technology entrepreneurship involves identifying and exploiting opportunities by leveraging technology to create innovative solutions. It goes beyond mere technological advancements and focuses on the crucial role of entrepreneurs in driving change and creating value. These individuals possess a unique set of skills, knowledge, and mindset that enable them to navigate the complexities of the technology-driven market.

One of the key characteristics of technology entrepreneurship is its disruptive nature. Technology entrepreneurs challenge existing norms, disrupt traditional industries, and create new markets. They introduce groundbreaking products, services, or business models that revolutionize the way things are done. By harnessing the power of technology, these entrepreneurs have the ability to transform entire industries and reshape the world as we know it.

Another defining characteristic of technology entrepreneurship is its relentless pursuit of innovation. Technology entrepreneurs are driven by a constant desire to push boundaries, explore uncharted territories, and find solutions to unsolved problems. They are not content with the status quo and constantly seek ways to improve, innovate, and create value. This relentless pursuit of innovation is what sets technology entrepreneurship apart from other forms of entrepreneurship.

Flexibility and adaptability are also crucial characteristics of successful technology entrepreneurs. In an ever-evolving technological landscape, they must be able to adapt quickly to changing market conditions, emerging trends, and new technologies. Being open to experimentation, learning from failures, and embracing uncertainty are essential traits for technology entrepreneurs to thrive in this dynamic environment.

Furthermore, technology entrepreneurship is often characterized by a strong focus on scalability and growth. Technology entrepreneurs have a vision to scale their innovations globally, reaching a wide audience and maximizing their impact. They strive to build scalable business models that can quickly grow and capture significant market share.

In conclusion, technology entrepreneurship is a dynamic and transformative force that drives innovation, disrupts industries, and shapes the future. Its characteristics of being disruptive, innovative, adaptable, and growth-oriented make it a fascinating field for entrepreneurs and innovators to explore. By understanding the essence of technology entrepreneurship, individuals in the fields of entrepreneurship and innovation can gain valuable insights and inspiration to make a lasting impact in the world.

The Role of Technology Entrepreneurs in Society

In today's fast-paced and ever-evolving world, technology entrepreneurs play a crucial role in shaping the society we live in. These disruptive innovators are individuals who have the vision, drive, and passion to create and implement groundbreaking technologies that transform industries, improve lives, and change the world as we know it.

Technology entrepreneurs are at the forefront of driving innovation and progress. They are the ones who identify gaps in existing systems, processes, or products and come up with revolutionary ideas to address these challenges. Through their entrepreneurial ventures, they bring about technological advancements that have far-reaching implications for society, economy, and overall human development.

One of the primary roles of technology entrepreneurs is to create opportunities for economic growth and job creation. By introducing innovative products or services, they stimulate market demand, attract investments, and foster entrepreneurship ecosystems. These entrepreneurs not only generate employment for themselves but also create job opportunities for others, contributing to economic stability and prosperity.

Moreover, technology entrepreneurs are catalysts for social change. They use their technological expertise and entrepreneurial mindset to address pressing societal issues such as healthcare, education, sustainability, and poverty alleviation. Through their disruptive innovations, they develop solutions that enhance access, affordability, and efficiency in various sectors, ultimately improving the quality of life for individuals and communities.

Furthermore, technology entrepreneurs are instrumental in fostering a culture of entrepreneurship and innovation. They inspire and motivate others to think creatively, take risks, and pursue their entrepreneurial aspirations. By sharing their success stories, failures, and lessons learned, they contribute to the knowledge and skill development of aspiring entrepreneurs. In doing so, they create a network of like-minded individuals who collaborate and share resources, further fueling the entrepreneurial ecosystem.

In conclusion, technology entrepreneurs play a vital role in society by driving innovation, creating economic opportunities, addressing social challenges, and fostering a culture of entrepreneurship and innovation. Their disruptive ideas and ventures have the power to reshape industries, improve lives, and make the world a better place. As technology continues to advance at an unprecedented pace, the role of these entrepreneurs becomes even more critical, as they are the ones who will shape the future and lead us towards a more prosperous and sustainable society.

Key Skills and Traits of Successful Technology Entrepreneurs

In the rapidly evolving landscape of technology entrepreneurship, certain skills and traits have proven to be crucial for success. Whether you are an aspiring entrepreneur or simply interested in the world of innovation, understanding these key qualities can provide valuable insights into what it takes to thrive in this field.

1. Vision and Creativity: Successful technology entrepreneurs possess a strong vision for the future and the ability to think outside the box. They have the foresight to identify emerging trends and envision innovative solutions to existing problems. Their creative thinking allows them to see opportunities where others see obstacles, leading to groundbreaking ideas and products.

2. Resilience and Adaptability: The technology industry is known for its fast-paced nature and constant change. Entrepreneurs must be resilient and adaptable, as they will inevitably face setbacks and challenges along the way. The ability to bounce back from failure, learn from mistakes, and pivot when necessary is crucial for long-term success.

3. Technical Expertise: While not all successful technology entrepreneurs are necessarily technical experts themselves, they have a strong understanding of the technical aspects of their business. They are able to communicate effectively with their technical team and make informed decisions that align with their overall vision.

4. Business Acumen: In addition to technical expertise, entrepreneurs need a solid foundation in business and finance. They understand how to create a viable business model, develop a sustainable revenue stream, and effectively manage resources. This combination of

technical and business knowledge enables them to make strategic decisions that drive growth and profitability.

5. Passion and Perseverance: Building a successful technology startup requires relentless passion and perseverance. Entrepreneurs must be willing to put in long hours, stay committed to their goals, and overcome obstacles with determination. Their unwavering belief in their vision and their ability to inspire others is what helps them navigate the ups and downs of entrepreneurship.

6. Networking and Collaboration: Technology entrepreneurs understand the power of building strong networks. They actively seek opportunities to connect with mentors, investors, industry experts, and potential partners. By fostering collaborative relationships, they gain access to invaluable resources, knowledge, and support that can accelerate their growth.

7. Continuous Learning: Successful entrepreneurs never stop learning. They stay updated with the latest industry trends, technologies, and market dynamics. They are curious and constantly seek opportunities to expand their knowledge and skillset. This continuous learning mindset allows them to stay ahead of the curve and make informed decisions.

In conclusion, the world of technology entrepreneurship demands a unique set of skills and traits. From visionary thinking to technical expertise, and from resilience to continuous learning, successful entrepreneurs possess a diverse range of qualities that enable them to thrive in this rapidly changing field. By embracing and cultivating these traits, aspiring entrepreneurs can increase their chances of making a meaningful impact in the world of innovation and entrepreneurship.

Chapter 3: The Disruptive Innovators' Mindset

Embracing Risk and Uncertainty

In the fast-paced world of entrepreneurship and innovation, risk and uncertainty are two constants that cannot be avoided. In fact, they are the very elements that set technology entrepreneurs apart from the rest. In this subchapter, we will explore the importance of embracing risk and uncertainty in the pursuit of disruptive innovation and changing the world.

Entrepreneurs are known for their ability to take risks. They understand that without risk, there can be no reward. It is this willingness to step outside of their comfort zones and push the boundaries of what is considered possible that allows them to create groundbreaking technologies and businesses. Embracing risk means being comfortable with the unknown, accepting that failure may be part of the journey, and being resilient enough to bounce back and learn from setbacks.

Uncertainty is another fundamental aspect of the entrepreneurial journey. Technology entrepreneurs are often venturing into uncharted territories, where there are no guarantees of success. They have to navigate through ambiguity, make decisions based on incomplete information, and adapt quickly to changing circumstances. Embracing uncertainty means having faith in one's abilities, being adaptable, and having the courage to make bold moves when necessary.

One of the reasons why technology entrepreneurs are able to embrace risk and uncertainty is their unique mindset. They see challenges as opportunities, failures as learning experiences, and setbacks as stepping stones towards success. They have a growth mindset, constantly seeking new knowledge and skills to overcome obstacles. This mindset allows them to view risk and uncertainty as necessary components of the innovation process, rather than obstacles to be avoided.

Embracing risk and uncertainty also requires a certain level of self-belief and confidence. Entrepreneurs understand that they are charting their own paths and may face criticism or skepticism from others. However, they have the self-assurance to stay true to their vision and persevere despite the naysayers. They believe in their abilities to create change and are willing to take the necessary risks to bring their ideas to life.

In conclusion, embracing risk and uncertainty is a crucial aspect of entrepreneurship and innovation. It is what sets technology entrepreneurs apart from the rest and allows them to disrupt industries and change the world. By accepting risk, navigating uncertainty, and adopting a growth mindset, entrepreneurs can forge ahead on their journey towards creating groundbreaking technologies and businesses. So, if you aspire to be a technology entrepreneur, remember to embrace risk and uncertainty, as they are the stepping stones to your success.

Challenging the Status Quo

Challenging the Status Quo: Embracing Disruption and Innovation

In the ever-evolving world of entrepreneurship and innovation, challenging the status quo has become a mantra for disruptive innovators who aim to change the world. In this subchapter, we will explore the importance of questioning established norms, embracing disruption, and the role of technology entrepreneurs in driving change.

The status quo represents the existing state of affairs, the conventional wisdom, and the established ways of doing things. While it may provide stability and predictability, it can also be a breeding ground for complacency and stagnation. Disruptive innovators, however, refuse to accept things as they are and instead seek to challenge and transform the existing order.

Disruption, often fueled by technology, has become the hallmark of these trailblazing entrepreneurs. They recognize that the world is constantly changing, and in order to stay relevant, they must constantly reinvent themselves and their businesses. They thrive on the uncertainty and chaos that disruption brings, as it presents new opportunities for growth and innovation.

Technology entrepreneurs play a pivotal role in challenging the status quo. With their bold visions and groundbreaking ideas, they introduce disruptive technologies that revolutionize industries, redefine business models, and change the way we live and work. They are driven by a desire to solve complex problems and create a positive impact on society.

By challenging the status quo, entrepreneurs are not only transforming industries but also inspiring others to think differently and embrace change. They encourage individuals and organizations to question long-held beliefs, challenge conventional wisdom, and step out of their comfort zones. In doing so, they foster a culture of innovation that fuels progress and propels societies forward.

However, challenging the status quo is not without its challenges. It requires courage, resilience, and a willingness to take risks. It means overcoming resistance, skepticism, and the fear of failure. But the rewards are immense – disruptive innovators have the power to shape the future, create new markets, and leave a lasting legacy.

In conclusion, the subchapter "Challenging the Status Quo" delves into the mindset of disruptive innovators who are changing the world through entrepreneurship and innovation. By questioning established norms, embracing disruption, and leveraging technology, these visionary individuals challenge the existing order and inspire others to think differently. They create a culture of innovation that propels societies forward and leaves a profound impact on the world. So, let us embrace the spirit of disruption, challenge the status quo, and become the change-makers who shape the future.

Thinking Big and Taking Action

In the realm of entrepreneurship and innovation, there is one key trait that sets successful individuals apart from the rest: the ability to think big and take action. This subchapter explores the power of thinking big and the importance of taking bold steps to make a lasting impact in the world of technology entrepreneurship.

Thinking big is about envisioning a future that others may not yet see. It involves having the audacity to dream beyond the boundaries of what is considered possible. By thinking big, entrepreneurs can identify opportunities that others overlook and create groundbreaking solutions that revolutionize industries.

One of the most iconic examples of thinking big and taking action is the story of Steve Jobs and Apple. Jobs had a vision of a world where technology seamlessly integrated into everyday life. He believed in creating products that were not only innovative but also beautifully designed. Through relentless determination and a refusal to settle for mediocrity, Jobs and his team transformed Apple into one of the most valuable and influential companies in the world.

Thinking big, however, is only the first step. Without action, ideas remain mere fantasies. Entrepreneurs must be willing to take calculated risks and step outside their comfort zones to bring their visions to life. This requires a combination of confidence, resilience, and a willingness to learn from failures.

Taking action often means challenging the status quo and embracing disruption. It involves pushing boundaries and questioning established norms. This disruptive mindset is what has fueled the success of countless technology entrepreneurs who have reshaped entire industries. From Elon Musk and his ambitious goals of colonizing Mars to Mark Zuckerberg and his mission to connect the world, these individuals have demonstrated the power of thinking big and taking bold action.

For everyone, regardless of their background or aspirations, thinking big and taking action can be a transformative mindset. It encourages individuals to pursue their passions, overcome obstacles, and leave a lasting impact on the world. Whether you aspire to start your own business or simply want to make a difference in your chosen field, thinking big and taking action is the driving force behind innovation and entrepreneurship.

In conclusion, thinking big and taking action are the cornerstones of disruptive innovation. By daring to dream big and having the courage to act on those dreams, entrepreneurs can change the world. This subchapter serves as a reminder to all readers that they too have the potential to think big and make a difference. By embracing this mindset, we can unlock our full potential and become the disruptive innovators of tomorrow.

Chapter 4: Identifying Disruptive Opportunities

Identifying Emerging Technologies

In the fast-paced world of entrepreneurship and innovation, staying ahead of the curve is crucial. Technology is constantly evolving, and new advancements have the power to disrupt industries and reshape the business landscape. To thrive in this dynamic environment, it is essential for entrepreneurs and innovators to identify emerging technologies early on. This subchapter will guide you through the process of recognizing and leveraging these game-changing innovations.

The first step in identifying emerging technologies is to stay informed. Keeping up with the latest industry news, attending conferences, and connecting with experts in the field will provide you with valuable insights into emerging trends. Engaging in online forums and communities dedicated to technology entrepreneurship can also offer a wealth of information and foster collaboration with like-minded individuals.

Additionally, cultivating a mindset of curiosity and foresight is crucial. By continuously questioning current practices and envisioning future possibilities, you can spot potential opportunities where emerging technologies can be applied. It is important to be open-minded and embrace experimentation, as this will enable you to explore and evaluate new technologies effectively.

A key aspect of identifying emerging technologies is understanding the market demand and potential impact. Conducting market research and analyzing consumer behavior can help you identify the needs and pain points that emerging technologies can address. By aligning these technologies with market demands, you can develop innovative solutions that have the potential to disrupt existing industries or create entirely new markets.

Collaboration and partnerships are also essential when it comes to identifying emerging technologies. Networking with industry leaders, entrepreneurs, and researchers can provide you with valuable insights and access to cutting-edge technologies. By building relationships with key players in the field, you can gain access to early-stage technologies and even participate in collaborative research and development efforts.

Furthermore, monitoring the activities of startups and venture capitalists can offer valuable clues about emerging technologies. These entities are often at the forefront of innovation, investing in and developing technologies that have the potential to revolutionize industries. By tracking their investments and acquisitions, you can identify emerging technologies that are gaining traction and likely to shape the future.

In conclusion, identifying emerging technologies is a crucial skill for entrepreneurs and innovators in today's rapidly evolving world. By staying informed, fostering curiosity, understanding market demands, collaborating with key players, and monitoring startup activities, you can position yourself at the forefront of technological innovation. Embrace the opportunities that emerging technologies present, and you will pave the way for disruptive innovation and change the world with your entrepreneurial endeavors.

Understanding Market Needs and Gaps

In the fast-paced world of entrepreneurship and innovation, one crucial aspect that sets successful technology entrepreneurs apart is their ability to identify and understand market needs and gaps. These disruptors possess a unique skill set that enables them to identify the unmet needs of consumers and develop innovative solutions to address those gaps. This subchapter delves into the importance of understanding market needs and gaps and provides valuable insights for entrepreneurs and innovators of all backgrounds.

Market needs and gaps refer to the unfulfilled demands and opportunities that exist within a particular industry or market. Identifying these gaps is the first step towards creating disruptive innovations that can change the world. By understanding the needs and pain points of potential customers, entrepreneurs can develop products and services that provide significant value and solve real-world problems.

To effectively understand market needs and gaps, entrepreneurs must adopt a customer-centric approach. This involves conducting thorough market research, engaging with potential customers, and actively listening to their feedback. By immersing themselves in the target market, entrepreneurs can gain a deep understanding of customer preferences, desires, and pain points. This knowledge serves as the foundation for developing groundbreaking solutions that meet these needs and bridge the gaps.

In addition to understanding customer needs, entrepreneurs must also assess the competitive landscape. This involves analyzing existing solutions, identifying their limitations, and spotting areas where improvements can be made. By studying the competition, entrepreneurs can gain valuable insights into market trends, customer expectations, and potential gaps that have yet to be addressed.

Furthermore, understanding market needs and gaps requires entrepreneurs to stay up-to-date with industry trends and emerging technologies. By staying informed about the latest advancements, entrepreneurs can proactively anticipate future needs and position themselves as industry leaders. This knowledge also enables entrepreneurs to leverage emerging technologies to create innovative solutions that surpass existing offerings.

Ultimately, understanding market needs and gaps is the key to disruptive innovation. By identifying unmet needs and developing solutions that address those gaps, entrepreneurs have the potential to revolutionize industries and change the world. This subchapter aims to equip aspiring entrepreneurs and innovators with the knowledge and mindset required to identify and understand market needs and gaps, empowering them to create transformative technologies that have a lasting impact. Whether you are a seasoned entrepreneur or someone looking to embark on an entrepreneurial journey, this subchapter will provide valuable insights and guidance to help you navigate the ever-changing landscape of entrepreneurship and innovation.

Analyzing Industry Disruptions and Trends

In today's rapidly evolving world, it is crucial for entrepreneurs and innovators to stay ahead of the curve by analyzing industry disruptions and trends. In this subchapter, we will delve into the importance of understanding these disruptions and explore how technology entrepreneurs are changing the world.

Industry disruptions can occur due to various factors such as technological advancements, changing consumer preferences, and regulatory changes. By analyzing these disruptions, entrepreneurs can identify emerging trends and seize opportunities to create innovative solutions that cater to evolving market demands.

One of the key aspects of analyzing industry disruptions is staying updated with the latest technological advancements. Technology is driving major changes in various industries, from healthcare and finance to transportation and communication. By closely monitoring emerging technologies such as artificial intelligence, blockchain, and the Internet of Things, entrepreneurs can identify ways to leverage these advancements and disrupt traditional business models.

Furthermore, understanding consumer preferences is essential for identifying industry disruptions. Consumer behavior is constantly evolving, driven by factors such as changing demographics, social trends, and economic shifts. Entrepreneurs who can anticipate these changes and adapt their products or services accordingly will have a competitive edge in the market.

Moreover, entrepreneurs need to be aware of regulatory changes that can disrupt industries. Government policies and regulations can significantly impact industries, either by creating opportunities or imposing hurdles for entrepreneurs. By keeping a close eye on legislative changes, entrepreneurs can proactively adapt their strategies and business models to navigate these disruptions effectively.

In the book "Disruptive Innovators: How Technology Entrepreneurs Are Changing the World," we explore real-life examples of entrepreneurs who have successfully analyzed industry disruptions and harnessed them to create groundbreaking innovations. These stories serve as an inspiration for aspiring entrepreneurs and provide valuable insights into the strategies and mindset required to drive disruptive change.

Whether you are an experienced entrepreneur or someone interested in the world of innovation, understanding industry disruptions and trends is crucial for sustained success. By analyzing disruptions, entrepreneurs can identify gaps in the market, develop innovative solutions, and shape the future of industries. This subchapter will equip you with the knowledge and tools to navigate the ever-changing landscape of entrepreneurship and innovation.

Chapter 5: Navigating the Innovation Process

Idea Generation and Validation

In the fast-paced world of entrepreneurship and innovation, the ability to generate and validate ideas is crucial for success. This subchapter will explore the processes and techniques that can help aspiring entrepreneurs and innovators in generating and validating their ideas effectively.

The first step in idea generation is to foster a creative and open mindset. This involves challenging conventional thinking and embracing new possibilities. Entrepreneurs need to be curious and willing to explore uncharted territories. They should actively seek inspiration from diverse sources, such as industry trends, customer needs, and emerging technologies.

Brainstorming sessions are a popular method for generating ideas. By gathering a diverse group of individuals, entrepreneurs can tap into different perspectives and experiences. Encouraging open and non-judgmental discussions can lead to the emergence of innovative and disruptive ideas. It is important to create an environment where participants feel comfortable sharing their thoughts freely.

Once ideas are generated, the next step is to validate their potential. This involves conducting market research and seeking feedback from potential customers. Entrepreneurs should identify their target audience and gather insights on their preferences, pain points, and needs. This information will help in refining and prioritizing ideas based on market demand.

Prototyping is another valuable tool for idea validation. By creating a minimum viable product (MVP), entrepreneurs can test the feasibility and desirability of their ideas. This iterative process allows for quick feedback and adjustments before investing significant resources.

Entrepreneurs should also consider the competitive landscape while validating their ideas. Understanding the existing market players and their offerings can help in identifying gaps and opportunities. By conducting a thorough analysis, entrepreneurs can position their ideas to stand out from the competition.

Validation should not be limited to external factors only. Self-reflection and feedback from mentors, advisors, and peers are equally important. Seeking constructive criticism can help in identifying blind spots and areas for improvement.

In conclusion, idea generation and validation are vital steps in the journey of an entrepreneur or innovator. By adopting a creative mindset, leveraging brainstorming sessions, conducting market research, prototyping, and seeking feedback, entrepreneurs can increase the chances of developing successful and disruptive ideas. Remember, innovation is not a one-time event but an ongoing process that requires continuous learning and adaptation.

Building a Minimum Viable Product (MVP)

In today's fast-paced technology-driven world, building a Minimum Viable Product (MVP) has become a crucial step for entrepreneurs and innovators looking to disrupt industries and change the world. The concept of an MVP is simple yet powerful - create a basic version of your product or service that solves a specific problem in the market, and iterate from there based on user feedback and data analysis.

For entrepreneurs and innovators in the niches of entrepreneurship and innovation, understanding the process of building an MVP is essential. It allows them to test their ideas quickly and efficiently, minimizing the risk of investing time and resources into a product that may not resonate with the market.

The first step in building an MVP is identifying the core problem or pain point that your product or service aims to solve. This requires thorough market research and a deep understanding of your target audience. By pinpointing the specific problem you are addressing, you can ensure that your MVP focuses on delivering a solution that is both valuable and feasible.

Once you have a clear problem statement, the next step is to design a simple and functional prototype of your product. This prototype should have the minimum features necessary to solve the identified problem effectively. It is important to avoid feature bloat at this stage, as it can lead to unnecessary complexity and delays in development.

With a prototype in hand, it's time to gather feedback from potential users and customers. This can be done through user testing, surveys, or focus groups. The goal is to gather insights that will help you refine and improve your MVP. Pay attention to user feedback and iterate on your product accordingly.

The key to building a successful MVP lies in the ability to balance speed and quality. While it is important to release your MVP quickly to test the market, it is equally crucial to ensure that the product is of sufficient quality to provide a positive user experience. Finding this balance requires a lean and agile approach to development.

In conclusion, building a Minimum Viable Product is a crucial step for entrepreneurs and innovators seeking to disrupt industries and change the world. By identifying the core problem, designing a simple prototype, and gathering user feedback, you can iterate and improve your product until it meets the needs of the market. Embracing the concept of an MVP allows you to minimize risk, validate your ideas, and ultimately build a successful and impactful product or service.

Testing and Iterating

In the fast-paced world of entrepreneurship and innovation, testing and iterating are crucial components for success. The process of developing a disruptive innovation involves constant experimentation, refinement, and adaptation. In this subchapter, we will explore the importance of testing and iterating and how it has revolutionized the way technology entrepreneurs are changing the world.

Testing is an essential step in the innovation process. It allows entrepreneurs to gather valuable data, assess the viability of their ideas, and make informed decisions. By testing their assumptions, entrepreneurs can identify flaws, uncover new possibilities, and refine their solutions. Whether it's through market research, surveys, or prototype testing, entrepreneurs can gain valuable insights that guide their innovation journey.

However, testing alone is not enough. Iterating, or the process of making small incremental changes based on feedback and data, is equally important. With each iteration, entrepreneurs refine their ideas, products, or services, bringing them closer to perfection. The iterative approach enables entrepreneurs to learn from failures, adapt to changing market dynamics, and steadily improve their offerings.

The beauty of testing and iterating lies in its ability to minimize risks. Instead of investing significant resources into a single idea, entrepreneurs can take small steps, evaluate the results, and pivot if necessary. This iterative process allows entrepreneurs to fail fast and fail forward, maximizing their chances of success while minimizing the negative impact of failures.

Moreover, testing and iterating foster innovation and creativity. By constantly challenging assumptions and seeking feedback, entrepreneurs can push the boundaries of what is possible. This process encourages a culture of experimentation and continuous improvement, leading to groundbreaking innovations that disrupt industries and change the world.

In today's hyper-competitive business landscape, technology entrepreneurs cannot afford to develop products or services in isolation. Testing and iterating facilitate collaboration and engagement with customers, investors, and other stakeholders. By involving the target audience throughout the innovation process, entrepreneurs ensure that their solutions meet real needs and deliver value.

In conclusion, testing and iterating are fundamental pillars of successful entrepreneurship and innovation. By embracing these practices, entrepreneurs can validate their ideas, refine their offerings, minimize risks, foster innovation, and engage with their target audience effectively. The ability to test and iterate is what sets disruptive innovators apart, enabling them to change the world, one step at a time. Whether you are a seasoned entrepreneur or someone looking to embark on a tech startup journey, understanding and implementing testing and iterating principles will be critical to your success.

Scaling and Growth Strategies

In the fast-paced world of technology entrepreneurship, scaling and growth strategies are crucial for success. As disruptive innovators strive to change the world, they need to continuously evaluate and adjust their strategies to ensure their ventures thrive.

Scaling a business involves increasing its capacity to handle growth while maintaining efficiency and profitability. It requires careful planning, resource allocation, and a deep understanding of market dynamics. Entrepreneurs must consider several key factors when formulating their scaling strategies.

One vital aspect is identifying the right timing for scaling. Rushing into expansion without a solid foundation can lead to disastrous outcomes. Entrepreneurs must analyze their market, assess their product-market fit, and ensure they have a stable customer base before scaling. Additionally, they need to evaluate if their business model is scalable and adaptable to changing market conditions.

Finding the right growth strategy is equally critical. Different approaches may work for different entrepreneurs, depending on their goals and resources. Some may opt for organic growth, expanding gradually by reinvesting profits. Others may choose to seek external funding, either through venture capitalists, angel investors, or crowdfunding platforms. This route allows for faster growth but comes with its own set of challenges, including dilution of ownership and increased pressure to perform.

Entrepreneurs should also explore strategic partnerships and collaborations as growth strategies. Teaming up with complementary businesses can provide access to new markets, resources, and expertise. Joint ventures, licensing agreements, or mergers and acquisitions can be effective ways to expand operations rapidly.

Furthermore, embracing innovation and technology is fundamental for scaling businesses in today's digital era. Adopting emerging technologies, such as artificial intelligence, blockchain, or cloud computing, can streamline operations, enhance customer experiences, and open up new growth opportunities.

However, scaling brings its own set of challenges. Entrepreneurs must be prepared to face increased competition, higher customer expectations, and operational complexities. It is crucial to build a strong team, delegate responsibilities, and establish efficient processes to manage growth effectively.

In conclusion, scaling and growth strategies are indispensable for technology entrepreneurs aiming to disrupt industries and change the world. By carefully analyzing their market, timing their expansion, choosing the right growth strategy, and embracing innovation, entrepreneurs can navigate the challenges of scaling successfully. With a well-executed growth plan, they can propel their ventures to new heights, creating a lasting impact in the realms of entrepreneurship and innovation.

Chapter 6: Funding and Resources for Technology Entrepreneurs

Bootstrapping and Self-Funding

Bootstrapping and Self-Funding: Unlocking Entrepreneurial Potential

In the fast-paced world of entrepreneurship and innovation, one of the key challenges for aspiring tech entrepreneurs is securing adequate funding to turn their ideas into reality. However, there is a path less traveled by, one that empowers entrepreneurs to build their dreams from scratch without relying on external investors. This subchapter explores the concept of bootstrapping and self-funding, uncovering how it can be a game-changer for anyone looking to disrupt the status quo in their respective industries.

Bootstrapping refers to the practice of starting a business with minimal external capital and relying on one's own resources, creativity, and determination to succeed. This approach allows entrepreneurs to retain full control over their ventures, making strategic decisions independently and avoiding the pressures and compromises that external funding might bring.

Self-funding, on the other hand, involves using personal savings, credit cards, or loans to finance a business venture. It requires entrepreneurs to have confidence in their vision and the willingness to take calculated risks to bring their ideas to life. While it may involve personal sacrifices and careful financial planning, self-funding allows entrepreneurs to maintain ownership and stay true to their original vision.

Bootstrapping and self-funding are not only viable options for entrepreneurs lacking access to traditional funding sources but also a strategic choice for those who wish to build a sustainable business on their own terms. By embracing these approaches, entrepreneurs can build a strong foundation for their ventures, fostering innovation and creativity while staying true to their vision.

This subchapter explores various strategies and tactics that can help entrepreneurs bootstrap their businesses. It delves into the art of resourcefulness, showcasing how entrepreneurs can leverage their existing networks, skills, and knowledge to minimize costs and maximize efficiency. It also discusses the significance of lean methodologies, emphasizing how entrepreneurs can test their assumptions and iterate quickly to find a viable business model.

Furthermore, the subchapter highlights success stories of entrepreneurs who have successfully bootstrapped and self-funded their ventures, proving that limited resources should never be a deterrent to success. These stories inspire and empower aspiring entrepreneurs, demonstrating that with determination, creativity, and strategic thinking, anyone can overcome financial constraints and achieve their entrepreneurial goals.

In conclusion, bootstrapping and self-funding offer a unique pathway for entrepreneurs to disrupt the industry and change the world. This subchapter equips readers from all walks of life with the knowledge, tools, and inspiration to embrace these approaches, empowering them to unlock their entrepreneurial potential and make their mark on the world of innovation. Whether you are a seasoned entrepreneur or just starting your journey, the concepts explored here will undoubtedly reshape your perspective on funding and ignite the entrepreneurial fire within you.

Angel Investors and Venture Capitalists

In the world of entrepreneurship and innovation, securing funding is often a critical component of turning an idea into a reality. One common avenue for raising capital is through the support of angel investors and venture capitalists. These individuals and firms are known for their willingness to take risks on promising startups and emerging technologies, providing the necessary financial backing and guidance to help them grow and succeed.

Angel investors, often referred to as "angels," are typically wealthy individuals who invest their personal funds into early-stage companies. These individuals not only provide financial support but also bring their expertise, experience, and network to the table. Unlike traditional lenders, angel investors are willing to take on higher risks in exchange for potentially high returns on their investments. They often invest in sectors they are passionate about and may be more willing to support ideas that are considered unconventional or disruptive.

On the other hand, venture capitalists are professional investment firms that manage funds from various sources, such as high-net-worth individuals, pension funds, and corporations. Venture capitalists typically invest in startups that have already demonstrated the potential for rapid growth and profitability. They provide larger sums of capital compared to angel investors and often require a significant equity stake in return.

Both angel investors and venture capitalists play crucial roles in the startup ecosystem. They not only provide financial support but also offer valuable mentorship, access to industry connections, and strategic guidance. These investors bring a wealth of experience and knowledge in scaling businesses, navigating challenges, and maximizing opportunities.

For entrepreneurs, securing funding from angel investors or venture capitalists can be a game-changer. It allows them to accelerate their growth, hire talented employees, invest in research and development, and expand into new markets. Moreover, the involvement of these investors provides credibility and validation to the startup, making it easier to attract additional funding and partnerships.

However, it's important for entrepreneurs to carefully consider the implications of accepting external funding. Angel investors and venture capitalists often require a significant equity stake, which means giving up ownership and control of the company. Entrepreneurs must weigh the benefits of funding against the potential loss of autonomy and decision-making power.

In conclusion, angel investors and venture capitalists are vital players in the world of entrepreneurship and innovation. Their financial support, expertise, and network can be transformative for startups, enabling them to disrupt industries, create new markets, and change the world. Entrepreneurs must carefully evaluate the pros and cons of accepting external funding to ensure alignment with their long-term vision and goals.

Government Grants and Support Programs

In today's rapidly evolving world, innovation and entrepreneurship have become vital drivers of economic growth and social progress. Technology entrepreneurs, in particular, have been at the forefront of disruptive innovation, transforming industries and creating new possibilities. However, starting and running a successful tech venture can be challenging, especially when it comes to securing adequate funding. This is where government grants and support programs play a crucial role.

Government grants and support programs are designed to foster entrepreneurship and innovation by providing financial assistance, resources, and mentorship to individuals and organizations working on groundbreaking projects. These programs are available to a wide range of entrepreneurs, from startups to established companies, and they cover various sectors such as technology, healthcare, clean energy, and more.

One of the key advantages of government grants is that they offer a non-dilutive source of funding. Unlike venture capital or loans, which require giving up equity or incurring debt, grants provide entrepreneurs with the financial means to pursue their ideas without sacrificing ownership or taking on additional financial burdens. This allows entrepreneurs to focus on their innovation and business development, rather than worrying about immediate financial returns.

Moreover, government grants often come with additional benefits beyond financial support. Many programs provide access to valuable resources such as research facilities, testing labs, and networking opportunities. They also offer mentorship and guidance from experienced professionals, helping entrepreneurs navigate the complexities of the business world and increasing their chances of success.

For individuals and organizations interested in pursuing government grants, it is essential to understand the different programs available and their eligibility criteria. Governments at various levels - local, regional, and national - offer grants and support programs, each with its own focus areas and application requirements. Entrepreneurs should thoroughly research and identify the programs that align with their project goals and objectives.

Additionally, it is important to note that government grants are highly competitive. The application process often involves rigorous evaluation and selection, as funding agencies aim to invest in projects with the highest potential for impact and economic growth. Entrepreneurs must demonstrate the viability, scalability, and societal benefits of their ventures through a well-crafted business plan and compelling proposal.

In conclusion, government grants and support programs play a vital role in fostering entrepreneurship and innovation in the technology sector. By providing financial assistance, resources, and mentorship, these programs enable entrepreneurs to pursue their groundbreaking ideas without the immediate financial burdens associated with traditional funding sources. However, it is crucial for entrepreneurs to thoroughly research and understand the different programs available and to craft a compelling proposal to increase their chances of securing grant funding. With the right support, disruptive innovators can continue changing the world and driving economic and social progress.

Chapter 7: Building a Strong Team

Attracting and Retaining Top Talent

In today's fast-paced business world, attracting and retaining top talent is crucial for the success of any organization. As technology continues to evolve and disrupt various industries, entrepreneurs must adapt and find innovative ways to recruit and retain the best and brightest professionals.

Attracting top talent starts with creating a compelling vision and company culture that resonates with potential employees. Entrepreneurs need to clearly communicate their mission, values, and goals to showcase why their organization is unique and worth joining. People are often drawn to companies that have a clear purpose and a positive impact on society. By highlighting these aspects, entrepreneurs can attract individuals who are highly motivated and passionate about making a difference.

In addition to a compelling vision, entrepreneurs should offer competitive compensation packages and benefits. Top talent often seeks opportunities that not only provide financial stability but also offer growth prospects and work-life balance. Offering flexible working hours, remote work options, and professional development opportunities can be major attractions for potential candidates.

To retain top talent, entrepreneurs must create an inclusive and empowering work environment. Providing ongoing training and development opportunities can help employees feel valued and invested in their professional growth. Encouraging a culture of innovation where employees can contribute ideas and take ownership of their work can also foster a sense of belonging and loyalty.

Entrepreneurs should prioritize creating a positive company culture that promotes collaboration, open communication, and work-life balance. Employees who feel supported and appreciated are more likely to stay with an organization for the long term. Recognizing and rewarding exceptional performance can also help retain top talent and motivate others to excel.

Furthermore, entrepreneurs should invest in building strong relationships with their employees. Regular one-on-one meetings, mentorship programs, and team-building activities can help foster a sense of community and loyalty. By demonstrating a genuine interest in their employees' well-being and career progression, entrepreneurs can create an environment where top talent feels valued and supported.

In conclusion, attracting and retaining top talent is crucial for the success and growth of any organization, especially in the dynamic world of entrepreneurship and innovation. By creating a compelling vision, offering competitive compensation packages, and fostering an inclusive and empowering work environment, entrepreneurs can attract and retain the best professionals in their field. By investing in their employees' growth and well-being, entrepreneurs can build a talented and loyal team that will drive their organization's success in the ever-evolving business landscape.

Effective Leadership and Team Management

In the fast-paced world of entrepreneurship and innovation, effective leadership and team management are crucial skills that can make or break a company's success. In this subchapter, we will discuss the key principles and strategies that can empower entrepreneurs to become effective leaders and manage their teams efficiently.

Leadership is not about bossing people around; it is about inspiring and motivating individuals to achieve their full potential. Entrepreneurs need to lead by example, demonstrating a strong work ethic, passion for their vision, and the ability to adapt to changing circumstances. By embodying these qualities, entrepreneurs can inspire their teams to do the same.

One of the fundamental aspects of effective leadership is clear communication. Entrepreneurs must be able to articulate their vision, goals, and expectations to their team members. By ensuring that everyone is on the same page, entrepreneurs can create a cohesive and aligned team that works towards a common objective.

Additionally, effective leaders understand the importance of developing and nurturing their team members' skills. Entrepreneurs should identify the strengths and weaknesses of each individual and provide them with opportunities for growth and development. By investing in their team's professional development, entrepreneurs not only empower their employees but also build a stronger and more resilient organization.

Another crucial aspect of effective leadership is the ability to foster a positive and supportive work environment. Entrepreneurs should encourage open communication, collaboration, and a culture of trust within their teams. By creating a safe space for sharing ideas and feedback, entrepreneurs can harness the collective intelligence of their team and drive innovation.

In terms of team management, entrepreneurs need to delegate responsibilities effectively. Trusting and empowering team members to take ownership of their tasks not only lightens the entrepreneur's workload but also enables their team to develop a sense of ownership and accountability. Effective delegation allows entrepreneurs to focus on strategic decisions and higher-level tasks.

Furthermore, entrepreneurs should prioritize building a diverse and inclusive team. By embracing different perspectives, backgrounds, and experiences, entrepreneurs can foster creativity and innovation within their organization. Diverse teams are more likely to challenge the status quo, think outside the box, and come up with disruptive ideas.

In conclusion, effective leadership and team management are critical skills for entrepreneurs in the dynamic world of entrepreneurship and innovation. By embodying the principles discussed in this subchapter, entrepreneurs can inspire their teams, foster a positive work environment, and drive their organizations towards success.

Collaboration and Partnerships

In the fast-paced world of technology entrepreneurship, collaboration and partnerships have become essential for success. No longer can entrepreneurs rely solely on their own skills and resources. The ability to form strategic alliances and work together with other individuals and organizations has become a key factor in driving innovation and changing the world.

Collaboration opens up endless possibilities for entrepreneurs, allowing them to tap into a diverse range of knowledge, expertise, and resources. By working together, entrepreneurs can combine their strengths and leverage each other's networks, ultimately achieving far greater outcomes than they could on their own. Through collaboration, entrepreneurs can access new markets, gain access to specialized skills, and share the risks and costs associated with developing disruptive technologies.

Partnerships are particularly important in the world of technology entrepreneurship. Startups often face numerous challenges, including limited funding, market uncertainty, and resource scarcity. By forming partnerships with established companies, entrepreneurs can gain access to the necessary resources, such as funding, manufacturing capabilities, and distribution channels. These partnerships can provide startups with the much-needed support to scale their innovations and bring them to market faster.

Furthermore, collaborations and partnerships foster an environment of innovation and creativity. When entrepreneurs from different backgrounds and industries come together, they bring with them unique perspectives and ideas. By combining these diverse viewpoints, entrepreneurs can generate innovative solutions to complex problems.

Collaborations also encourage continuous learning and improvement, as entrepreneurs can learn from each other's experiences and mistakes.

In the ever-evolving entrepreneurial landscape, collaboration and partnerships are not limited to just individuals and organizations within the same industry. Entrepreneurs are increasingly forming cross-industry collaborations, bringing together experts from various fields to tackle common challenges. These collaborations foster disruptive innovation by combining technologies and expertise from different domains, resulting in groundbreaking solutions that can transform entire industries.

In conclusion, collaboration and partnerships are critical elements for technology entrepreneurs aiming to change the world. By working together, entrepreneurs can overcome challenges, access resources, and foster innovation. Whether it is forming strategic alliances with other startups or partnering with established companies, entrepreneurs can amplify their impact and accelerate their journey towards disruptive innovation. In this interconnected world, collaboration is not just a choice but a necessity for those who aim to drive change and shape the future.

Chapter 8: Overcoming Challenges and Failures

Dealing with Rejection and Setbacks

In the journey of entrepreneurship and innovation, one of the most challenging aspects is undoubtedly facing rejection and setbacks. Every entrepreneur, regardless of their level of success, has encountered numerous obstacles along the way. These obstacles, however, should not be viewed as roadblocks, but rather as stepping stones toward growth and success.

Rejection is an inevitable part of the entrepreneurial process. Whether it's a potential investor turning down your pitch or a customer declining your product, it's crucial to understand that rejection does not define you or your abilities. Instead of dwelling on the negative outcome, use rejection as an opportunity to learn and improve. Analyze the reasons behind the rejection, seek feedback, and identify areas that need refinement. Remember, even the most successful entrepreneurs faced rejection numerous times before achieving their breakthrough.

Setbacks, on the other hand, can feel discouraging and demotivating. It's important to remember that setbacks are temporary and can be overcome with the right mindset. Embrace setbacks as valuable learning experiences that can propel you forward. Take a step back, reevaluate your strategies, and identify the areas that need adjustment. Use setbacks as an opportunity to reassess your goals, refine your approach, and emerge even stronger.

To effectively deal with rejection and setbacks, it is essential to cultivate resilience and mental strength. Surround yourself with a support network of like-minded individuals who understand the challenges you face. Seek guidance from mentors who have experienced similar setbacks and learn from their wisdom. Remember that failure is not the opposite of success but rather a stepping stone on the path to success.

Resilience also involves maintaining a positive mindset. Instead of dwelling on failures, focus on the lessons learned and the opportunities they present. Embrace failure as a natural part of the entrepreneurial journey and recognize that each setback brings you one step closer to achieving your goals.

Additionally, it's crucial to practice self-care during challenging times. Take breaks, exercise, and engage in activities that rejuvenate your spirit. Surround yourself with positivity, whether through inspiring books, motivational podcasts, or uplifting conversations. Taking care of your mental and physical well-being will enhance your ability to tackle rejection and setbacks head-on.

In conclusion, rejection and setbacks are an inevitable part of the entrepreneurial journey. By reframing rejection as an opportunity for growth and setbacks as temporary hurdles, entrepreneurs can navigate these challenges with resilience and determination. Remember that every successful entrepreneur has faced rejection and setbacks, and it is through these experiences that they have honed their skills and achieved greatness. Embrace rejection, learn from setbacks, and never lose sight of your ultimate goal.

Learning from Mistakes and Pivoting

Mistakes are an inevitable part of any journey, particularly in the realm of entrepreneurship and innovation. However, what sets successful technology entrepreneurs apart is their ability to learn from these mistakes and pivot their strategies accordingly. In the subchapter "Learning from Mistakes and Pivoting," we delve into the invaluable lessons that can be gleaned from failures and the art of adaptation.

Entrepreneurship is a rollercoaster ride, with ups and downs that test even the most resilient individuals. But it is during the downs, the moments of failure and setback, that the true potential for growth and innovation lies. Instead of dwelling on the disappointment, successful entrepreneurs embrace their mistakes as learning opportunities. They analyze the causes, identify the missteps, and extract lessons that can shape their future endeavors. By cultivating a mindset of continuous improvement, they transform setbacks into stepping stones towards success.

Pivoting is a crucial aspect of the entrepreneurial journey. It involves adjusting one's business model, strategy, or product in response to market feedback or changing circumstances. The ability to adapt and pivot is what separates the disruptors from the rest. By staying agile and open-minded, entrepreneurs can seize emerging opportunities, even if it means deviating from their original vision.

Throughout this subchapter, we explore real-life examples of entrepreneurs who faced adversity, made mistakes, and successfully pivoted. We analyze how industry giants like Airbnb, Uber, and Netflix adapted their business models to meet changing consumer needs and market dynamics. By examining these case studies, readers gain valuable insights into the mindset and strategies that enable entrepreneurs to thrive in uncertain and rapidly evolving environments.

Furthermore, we provide practical advice on fostering a culture of learning from mistakes within a team or organization. We discuss strategies for encouraging risk-taking, embracing failure, and creating an environment where individuals feel safe to experiment and learn. By instilling a growth mindset and promoting a culture of continuous learning, organizations can foster resilience and adaptability, ultimately driving innovation and success.

"Learning from Mistakes and Pivoting" is an essential subchapter for anyone interested in the world of entrepreneurship and innovation. Whether you are a budding entrepreneur, a seasoned business professional, or simply curious about the dynamics of disruptive technology companies, this subchapter will equip you with the tools and insights to learn from mistakes, adapt to change, and ultimately succeed in a rapidly evolving landscape.

Maintaining Resilience and Perseverance

In the fast-paced world of entrepreneurship and innovation, maintaining resilience and perseverance is crucial for success. As technology entrepreneurs, we face numerous challenges and setbacks on the path to changing the world. This subchapter aims to provide you, the reader, with valuable insights and strategies to help you stay resilient and persevere through the toughest of times.

Resilience is the ability to bounce back from failure or adversity. It is about staying strong and maintaining a positive mindset even when faced with obstacles. One key aspect of resilience is having a clear vision and purpose. When you have a strong sense of purpose, setbacks become mere hurdles on the road to success. It is important to remind yourself of your goals and the impact you aim to create in the world. This will provide you with the motivation and resilience needed to keep pushing forward.

Another important aspect of maintaining resilience is building a strong support network. Surrounding yourself with like-minded individuals who share your passion for entrepreneurship and innovation can be invaluable. They can provide support, guidance, and even act as a sounding board for your ideas. Additionally, seeking mentorship from experienced entrepreneurs who have faced similar challenges can offer valuable insights and help you navigate through difficult times.

Perseverance is the ability to keep going even when faced with repeated failures. It is about staying committed to your goals and not giving up. One key strategy for maintaining perseverance is embracing failure as a learning opportunity. Each setback provides an opportunity to learn, grow, and improve. It is important to analyze what went wrong, adapt your strategies, and try again. Remember, some of the most successful entrepreneurs have experienced numerous failures before achieving their breakthrough.

Moreover, practicing self-care and maintaining a healthy work-life balance is essential for staying resilient and persevering. Burnout can hinder your ability to think creatively and make sound decisions. Taking regular breaks, exercising, and pursuing hobbies outside of work can rejuvenate your mind and keep you motivated.

In conclusion, maintaining resilience and perseverance is vital for technology entrepreneurs looking to change the world. By having a clear vision, building a support network, embracing failure, and practicing self-care, you can overcome challenges and stay focused on your goals. Remember, the journey of an entrepreneur is filled with ups and downs, but it is your resilience and perseverance that will ultimately lead you to success in the ever-evolving world of entrepreneurship and innovation.

Chapter 9: Ethical Considerations in Technology Entrepreneurship

Balancing Profit and Social Impact

In today's fast-paced and interconnected world, entrepreneurship and innovation have become vital drivers of economic growth and social change. The rise of technology entrepreneurs has revolutionized various industries, presenting opportunities to tackle pressing societal issues while generating profits. This subchapter delves into the crucial concept of balancing profit and social impact, exploring how technology entrepreneurs are changing the world in a way that benefits everyone.

Entrepreneurs are often seen as profit-driven individuals solely focused on maximizing their financial gains. However, the landscape has shifted significantly over the years. A new breed of disruptors has emerged, driven by a desire to make a positive impact on society alongside their pursuit of profitability. These individuals recognize that business success is not solely defined by financial metrics but also by the positive change they can bring to communities and the environment.

By embracing innovation and leveraging technology, these entrepreneurs are developing groundbreaking solutions to address social and environmental challenges. They are creating products, services, and business models that are not only economically viable but also sustainable and socially responsible. Whether it is designing renewable energy systems, revolutionizing healthcare delivery, or fostering inclusive education, technology entrepreneurs are reshaping industries while making a lasting impact on society.

Balancing profit and social impact is a delicate task. Entrepreneurs must navigate the challenges associated with limited resources, market pressures, and societal expectations. However, by adopting a long-term perspective and incorporating social impact into their business strategies, entrepreneurs can create sustainable models that benefit both their bottom line and the greater good.

Furthermore, the alignment of profit and social impact is not only a moral imperative but also a strategic advantage. Today's consumers and investors are increasingly conscious of the social and environmental impact of their choices. They are more likely to support businesses that demonstrate a commitment to social responsibility. As such, technology entrepreneurs who prioritize social impact can attract a loyal customer base, gain investor confidence, and foster a positive brand image.

In conclusion, the subchapter "Balancing Profit and Social Impact" explores the significant role that technology entrepreneurs play in driving positive change and reshaping industries. By embracing innovation and incorporating social impact into their business strategies, these disruptors are not only generating profits but also leaving a lasting impact on society. Balancing profit and social impact is a delicate endeavor, but when done correctly, it can lead to long-term success, as more consumers and investors prioritize businesses that prioritize the greater good. As we delve deeper into the chapters of this book, we will explore inspiring examples of technology entrepreneurs who have successfully balanced profit and social impact, paving the way for a more sustainable and inclusive future.

Privacy and Data Security

In today's digital age, the protection of privacy and data security has become a critical concern for individuals and organizations alike. As technology entrepreneurs continue to disrupt traditional industries and change the world, it is imperative that they prioritize privacy and data security in their endeavors.

In this subchapter, we will delve into the importance of privacy and data security in the context of entrepreneurship and innovation. We will explore the potential risks associated with the collection, storage, and use of personal information, and discuss strategies for safeguarding sensitive data.

In an interconnected world where personal information is constantly shared and stored electronically, entrepreneurs must recognize the value of privacy and the potential consequences of data breaches. Whether it is customer information, intellectual property, or trade secrets, failure to protect sensitive data can result in devastating consequences, including financial loss, reputational damage, and even legal ramifications.

Entrepreneurs must adopt a proactive approach to privacy and data security. This involves implementing robust security measures, such as encryption, access controls, and regular audits, to ensure that data is protected from unauthorized access or disclosure. Additionally, entrepreneurs should educate themselves and their teams about the latest threats and best practices in the field of data security.

Meticulous attention should be given to privacy policies and terms of service agreements, ensuring that they are transparent and provide individuals with control over their personal information.

Entrepreneurs should also consider obtaining proper consent before collecting and using personal data, while adhering to relevant laws and regulations.

Moreover, entrepreneurs can benefit from collaborating with privacy and cybersecurity experts who can provide guidance and assist in the development of effective privacy and data security strategies. By investing in privacy and data security, entrepreneurs can not only protect their customers and stakeholders but also build trust and credibility, which are vital for long-term success.

In conclusion, privacy and data security are paramount considerations for entrepreneurs and innovators. Protecting sensitive data should be an integral part of any entrepreneurial venture, regardless of the industry or niche. By prioritizing privacy and implementing robust data security measures, entrepreneurs can foster a safe and trustworthy environment for their stakeholders, gain a competitive edge, and ultimately shape a world where innovation flourishes securely.

Ethical Use of Emerging Technologies

In this digital era, technology is evolving at an unprecedented pace, presenting entrepreneurs and innovators with an array of exciting opportunities. However, with great power comes great responsibility. The ethical use of emerging technologies is a crucial consideration that entrepreneurs and innovators must prioritize to ensure a positive impact on society.

The rapid advancements in technology, from artificial intelligence and blockchain to virtual reality and bioengineering, hold immense potential for transforming industries and solving complex problems. But as entrepreneurs, we must be mindful of the ethical implications of these technologies and their potential consequences.

One of the key ethical considerations is privacy and data protection. With the increasing reliance on technology, vast amounts of personal data are being collected, stored, and analyzed. Entrepreneurs must ensure that they handle this data responsibly, respecting individuals' privacy rights, and implementing robust security measures to prevent data breaches.

Another crucial aspect is the potential for bias and discrimination in emerging technologies. As entrepreneurs, we must be vigilant in addressing and mitigating any biases that may be embedded in algorithms or AI systems. It is essential to develop and deploy technologies that are fair, unbiased, and inclusive, ensuring equal opportunities for all individuals, regardless of their gender, race, or socioeconomic background.

Furthermore, entrepreneurs should consider the environmental impact of their innovations. As we strive to create groundbreaking technologies, we must also be mindful of sustainability and the responsible use of resources. By incorporating eco-friendly practices into our business models, we can contribute to a greener and more sustainable future for all.

Additionally, entrepreneurs should consider the ethical implications of automation and job displacement. While automation can increase efficiency and productivity, it can also lead to job losses and economic disparities. It is our responsibility to ensure that emerging technologies are designed to augment human capabilities rather than replace them, and to create new opportunities for employment and skill development.

In conclusion, the ethical use of emerging technologies is not just a moral imperative but also a strategic necessity for entrepreneurs and innovators. By embracing ethical principles, we can build trust with our customers, investors, and society at large. Let us be the disruptors who not only change the world but also do so responsibly, leaving a positive and lasting impact on the world of entrepreneurship and innovation.

Chapter 10: The Future of Disruptive Innovation

Emerging Technologies and Trends

In today's fast-paced world, technology is constantly evolving and shaping the way we live, work, and interact. As technology entrepreneurs continue to push the boundaries of innovation, the emergence of new technologies and trends has the potential to disrupt industries and transform our lives in unprecedented ways. In this subchapter, we will explore some of the most exciting emerging technologies and trends that are reshaping the landscape of entrepreneurship and innovation.

Artificial Intelligence (AI) is one of the most significant emerging technologies that has captured the imagination of entrepreneurs across various industries. With its ability to mimic human intelligence and automate complex tasks, AI has the potential to revolutionize sectors such as healthcare, finance, manufacturing, and transportation. From chatbots providing customer support to autonomous vehicles navigating our roads, AI is becoming an integral part of our daily lives.

The Internet of Things (IoT) is another transformative trend that is connecting devices and enabling seamless communication and data exchange. Entrepreneurs are leveraging IoT to create smart homes, cities, and industries, where everyday objects are interconnected, making our lives more convenient and efficient. From smart thermostats that adjust to our preferences to wearable devices that monitor our health, IoT is revolutionizing how we interact with our environment.

Blockchain technology, originally known for its association with cryptocurrencies like Bitcoin, is now being explored for its potential to revolutionize industries beyond finance. Entrepreneurs are harnessing the power of blockchain to create transparent and secure systems for supply chain management, healthcare records, and identity verification. Its decentralized nature and immutable record-keeping make blockchain a game-changer for industries that rely on trust and security.

The rise of renewable energy and sustainability is another significant trend that is reshaping the entrepreneurial landscape. With the increasing global concern over climate change, entrepreneurs are developing innovative solutions that harness the power of clean energy sources such as solar and wind. From solar-powered devices to energy-efficient buildings, sustainable technologies are not only reducing our carbon footprint but also creating new business opportunities.

As we delve into the world of emerging technologies and trends, it is important for entrepreneurs and innovators to stay informed and adaptable. The pace of technological advancements is accelerating, and those who can anticipate and leverage these disruptions will be at the forefront of driving change and creating new opportunities.

Whether you are an aspiring entrepreneur or simply curious about the future of technology, understanding these emerging technologies and trends is crucial. By embracing the potential of AI, IoT, blockchain, and sustainable solutions, we can shape a future that is more connected, efficient, and sustainable. The world of entrepreneurship and innovation is evolving, and it is up to us to seize the opportunities presented by these disruptive technologies and make a positive impact on the world we live in.

Global Impact and Opportunities

In today's rapidly changing world, technology entrepreneurs have emerged as the driving force behind disruptive innovation. Their ability to identify and capitalize on emerging trends has not only changed the way we live and work but has also created countless opportunities for individuals and societies around the globe. This subchapter, titled "Global Impact and Opportunities," explores the transformative power of technology entrepreneurship and its implications for everyone, particularly those interested in entrepreneurship and innovation.

One of the most significant impacts of technology entrepreneurs is their ability to democratize access to information and resources. Through innovative solutions and digital platforms, they have bridged the gap between developed and developing nations, providing equal opportunities for individuals to connect, learn, and thrive. This has led to the rise of a global entrepreneurial ecosystem, where talent and ideas can be shared and nurtured regardless of geographical boundaries. As a result, aspiring entrepreneurs from any corner of the world now have the chance to disrupt industries, create innovative products, and build successful businesses, leveling the playing field in the process.

Moreover, technology entrepreneurs are creating new markets and disrupting traditional industries, leading to economic growth and job creation. By identifying unmet needs and developing innovative solutions, they are not only transforming existing sectors but also creating entirely new industries. This presents a multitude of opportunities for individuals to start their own ventures, work on groundbreaking projects, and contribute to economic development on a global scale. The entrepreneurial mindset, coupled with technological advancements, has become a powerful catalyst for job creation and economic prosperity, providing individuals with the means to shape their own destinies.

The impact of technology entrepreneurship is not limited to economic growth; it extends to addressing critical global challenges as well. From healthcare to sustainability, technology entrepreneurs are leveraging their skills and resources to tackle pressing issues on a global scale. Through disruptive innovations, they are revolutionizing healthcare delivery, improving access to education, and developing sustainable solutions for a better future. Their ability to think outside the box and challenge the status quo has the potential to shape a more inclusive, sustainable, and prosperous world for all.

In conclusion, technology entrepreneurs have created a global impact and numerous opportunities for everyone. Their disruptive innovations have democratized access to information, transformed industries, and addressed critical global challenges. Whether you are an aspiring entrepreneur or simply interested in the world of innovation, understanding the power and potential of technology entrepreneurs is crucial. By embracing their mindset and exploring the opportunities they have created, individuals can contribute to shaping a brighter future for themselves and the world at large.

Inspiring the Next Generation of Technology Entrepreneurs

In today's rapidly evolving world, technology has become an integral part of our lives. From smartphones to artificial intelligence, technology has revolutionized the way we live, work, and interact. Behind these groundbreaking innovations are technology entrepreneurs who possess a unique combination of vision, passion, and determination to bring their ideas to life. As we navigate the digital age, it is crucial to inspire and nurture the next generation of technology entrepreneurs who will shape the future of our world.

Entrepreneurship and innovation go hand in hand. Entrepreneurs are the driving force behind disruptive ideas that challenge the status quo and push the boundaries of what is possible. They possess a relentless curiosity and a willingness to take risks, which sets them apart from the rest. Technology entrepreneurs, in particular, harness the power of cutting-edge technologies to create products and services that revolutionize industries, improve lives, and create new opportunities.

Inspiring the next generation of technology entrepreneurs is essential for several reasons. Firstly, technology entrepreneurship is a catalyst for economic growth. By encouraging and supporting young minds to explore their entrepreneurial potential, we can foster innovation and create a thriving ecosystem that generates jobs, fuels economic development, and drives societal progress.

Secondly, technology entrepreneurs have the power to solve some of the world's most pressing challenges. Whether it is developing sustainable energy solutions, improving healthcare access, or addressing social inequality, technology entrepreneurs have the potential to make a significant impact. By inspiring the next generation to leverage technology for the greater good, we can accelerate progress towards a more sustainable and inclusive future.

To inspire the next generation of technology entrepreneurs, it is essential to provide them with the right tools, resources, and mentorship. Educational institutions, governments, and industry leaders play a crucial role in fostering an entrepreneurial mindset and cultivating innovation. By offering entrepreneurship programs, internships, and mentorship opportunities, we can empower young individuals to unleash their creativity and transform their ideas into successful ventures.

Moreover, storytelling is a powerful tool to inspire and motivate aspiring technology entrepreneurs. Sharing the stories of successful technology entrepreneurs who have overcome challenges, transformed industries, and made a difference can ignite the spark of innovation in young minds. By showcasing diverse role models and highlighting their journeys, we can demonstrate that anyone, regardless of their background or circumstances, can become a technology entrepreneur.

In conclusion, inspiring the next generation of technology entrepreneurs is vital for driving economic growth, solving global challenges, and shaping a better future. By providing the right support, fostering an entrepreneurial mindset, and sharing inspiring stories, we can unlock the potential of young individuals and empower them to become the disruptive innovators of tomorrow. Together, let us create a world where technology entrepreneurship thrives, and innovation knows no bounds.

Chapter 11: Success Stories of Disruptive Innovators

Case Study 1: Company X Revolutionizes Industry Y

In the ever-evolving landscape of entrepreneurship and innovation, there are few stories as inspiring and impactful as that of Company X. This case study delves into the remarkable journey of a technology startup that revolutionized Industry Y, leaving an indelible mark on the business world.

Industry Y, once dominated by traditional giants, faced stagnation and resistance to change. Enter Company X, a group of young and visionary entrepreneurs who saw an opportunity to disrupt the status quo and reshape the industry through the power of technology.

The story begins with the founding members of Company X, who recognized a gap in the market and envisioned a solution that would not only address it but also redefine the way business was conducted. Armed with passion, determination, and a groundbreaking idea, they embarked on a journey that would challenge the norms and set new standards.

Through meticulous research and development, Company X introduced an innovative technology that streamlined processes, increased efficiency, and delivered unprecedented results. Their solution not only solved existing problems within Industry Y but also created new possibilities that were previously unimaginable.

The impact was felt across the entire ecosystem of Industry Y. Company X's disruptive technology empowered businesses to optimize their operations, reduce costs, and enhance their competitive edge. This newfound efficiency drove substantial growth, transforming not only individual companies but the industry as a whole.

But the success of Company X did not stop there. Their innovation sparked a ripple effect, inspiring other entrepreneurs and startups to think outside the box and challenge conventions. The industry witnessed a surge of creativity and innovation, leading to a wave of positive change that propelled it into a new era of progress.

The lessons learned from Company X's journey are invaluable to anyone interested in entrepreneurship and innovation. They exemplify the power of bold ideas, relentless determination, and a commitment to challenging the status quo. This case study serves as a testament to the fact that disruptive innovation knows no boundaries and that even the most entrenched industries can be transformed.

In conclusion, Company X's story is a testament to the transformative power of technology entrepreneurs. This case study highlights the importance of embracing change, thinking innovatively, and daring to challenge established norms. As technology continues to shape the world, it is entrepreneurs like those behind Company X who will lead the charge towards a brighter and more innovative future.

Case Study 2: Entrepreneur Z Disrupts the Market with Innovative Solution

In the fast-paced world of entrepreneurship and innovation, there are individuals who possess a unique ability to identify gaps in the market and create groundbreaking solutions. One such individual is Entrepreneur Z, who has disrupted the industry with an innovative solution that has changed the game for businesses and consumers alike.

Entrepreneur Z's journey began with a deep passion for solving complex problems and a relentless drive to make a difference. Recognizing the need for a more efficient and user-friendly solution in a particular industry, Z embarked on a mission to disrupt the market and create a product that would revolutionize the way businesses operate.

Through extensive research and collaboration with experts in the field, Entrepreneur Z developed an innovative solution that combined cutting-edge technology with intuitive design. This solution addressed the pain points experienced by businesses and consumers, providing them with a seamless and streamlined experience.

The impact of Entrepreneur Z's solution was immediately felt across the market. Businesses that adopted the solution experienced increased productivity, reduced costs, and improved customer satisfaction. Consumers, on the other hand, benefited from enhanced convenience, accessibility, and overall user experience.

What sets Entrepreneur Z apart from others in the industry is not just the innovative solution itself, but also the strategic approach taken to disrupt the market. Z recognized the importance of building strong partnerships with key stakeholders, leveraging their expertise and resources to scale the solution rapidly.

In addition, Entrepreneur Z embraced a culture of continuous learning and adaptation. Z understood that success in the dynamic landscape of entrepreneurship and innovation requires the ability to pivot and evolve in response to changing market demands. This mindset allowed Z to stay ahead of the competition and maintain a cutting-edge position in the industry.

Entrepreneur Z's disruptive innovation serves as an inspiration to aspiring entrepreneurs and innovators. It highlights the power of identifying market gaps, developing innovative solutions, and leveraging strategic partnerships to drive meaningful change. Z's success story demonstrates that with determination, creativity, and a deep understanding of customer needs, anyone can make a significant impact in the world of entrepreneurship and innovation.

In conclusion, Entrepreneur Z's journey showcases the transformative power of disruptive innovation. By addressing market gaps with innovative solutions, Z has not only changed the game for businesses and consumers but has also inspired a new generation of entrepreneurs and innovators to challenge the status quo and change the world.

Chapter 12: Conclusion

Recap of Key Concepts

In this subchapter, we will recap some of the key concepts discussed throughout the book "Disruptive Innovators: How Technology Entrepreneurs Are Changing the World." Whether you are an aspiring entrepreneur, a seasoned business owner, or simply interested in the world of entrepreneurship and innovation, this recap will help solidify your understanding of the essential concepts covered.

1. Disruptive Innovation: The concept of disruptive innovation lies at the core of this book. It refers to the process by which new technologies and business models disrupt existing industries, creating new markets and value networks. Disruptive innovators challenge traditional business models and capitalize on emerging trends to transform industries.

2. Mindset Shift: Successful technology entrepreneurs possess a unique mindset. They embrace risk, uncertainty, and failure as opportunities for growth. They are open to exploring unconventional ideas and are willing to challenge the status quo. Cultivating an entrepreneurial mindset is crucial for anyone looking to make a mark in the world of business.

3. Market Fit: Understanding the market and identifying a problem that needs solving is fundamental to successful entrepreneurship. Entrepreneurs must conduct thorough market research to identify gaps and unmet needs. By creating innovative solutions that resonate with the target audience, entrepreneurs can achieve market fit, ensuring their products or services align with customer demands.

4. Lean Startup Methodology: The lean startup methodology emphasizes quick experimentation and iterative product development. This approach encourages entrepreneurs to build minimum viable products (MVPs) and gather customer feedback early on. Through the build-measure-learn feedback loop, entrepreneurs can make informed decisions, refine their offerings, and avoid wasting time and resources on ideas that might not work.

5. Scaling: Scaling a business involves expanding operations to reach a larger customer base and increase revenue. Entrepreneurs must develop effective scaling strategies to sustain growth and navigate challenges. This includes establishing scalable business models, building efficient processes, and attracting the right talent.

6. Collaborative Ecosystems: Technology entrepreneurs thrive in collaborative ecosystems that foster innovation. These ecosystems consist of entrepreneurs, investors, mentors, and support organizations that work together to provide resources, guidance, and networking opportunities. Building relationships within these ecosystems can significantly enhance an entrepreneur's chances of success.

By reviewing these key concepts, you have gained a solid foundation in entrepreneurship and innovation. Remember, the world of disruptive innovation is constantly evolving, and staying updated on the latest trends and best practices is essential. As you embark on your entrepreneurial journey or continue to explore the fascinating realm of technology entrepreneurship, always be open to learning, adapting, and embracing change.

Empowering Readers to Embrace Technology Entrepreneurship

In today's rapidly evolving world, technology entrepreneurship has become a powerful force driving innovation and shaping industries. The ability to harness technology to create disruptive solutions and transform traditional business models has proven to be a game-changer for entrepreneurs. In this subchapter, we will explore how readers can embrace technology entrepreneurship, providing insights and guidance for those interested in venturing into the realm of innovation and entrepreneurship.

Technology entrepreneurship offers immense opportunities for individuals from all walks of life. Whether you are a young professional seeking to make an impact, an experienced entrepreneur looking to pivot your business, or simply someone with a passion for innovation, this subchapter is for you. We will delve into the key principles and mindset required to become a successful technology entrepreneur.

One of the critical aspects of embracing technology entrepreneurship is developing a deep understanding of emerging technologies and their potential applications. From artificial intelligence to blockchain, the world of technology is constantly evolving, and entrepreneurs need to stay ahead of the curve. We will explore various technologies and their impact on different industries, equipping readers with the knowledge needed to identify opportunities and envision groundbreaking solutions.

Additionally, we will discuss the importance of cultivating an entrepreneurial mindset. Technology entrepreneurship requires individuals to be adaptable, resilient, and resourceful. We will provide practical strategies and advice on how to cultivate these qualities, empowering readers to overcome challenges and take calculated risks.

Furthermore, we will explore the role of innovation ecosystems in nurturing technology entrepreneurship. From incubators and accelerators to collaboration networks and funding opportunities, these ecosystems provide invaluable support for entrepreneurs. We will guide readers on how to tap into these resources, connecting them with the right people and organizations to propel their ideas forward.

Finally, we will showcase inspiring stories and case studies of successful technology entrepreneurs who have changed the world through their innovations. By studying their journeys, readers will gain valuable insights into the mindset, strategies, and actions that led to their success.

Whether you are an aspiring entrepreneur or simply fascinated by the world of innovation, this subchapter will empower you to embrace technology entrepreneurship. By providing a comprehensive understanding of the subject and practical guidance, we aim to inspire readers to take the leap and become disruptors in their chosen fields. The future belongs to those who can harness technology to create positive change, and this subchapter will equip you with the tools to do just that.